The Official

Freebies

for

Fans

By the Editors of *Freebies* Magazine

Illustrations by Catherine Leary

Lowell House
Juvenile
Los Angeles

CONTEMPORARY
BOOKS
Chicago

Lowell House Juvenile
2029 Century Park East, Suite 3290
Los Angeles, CA 90067

Publisher: Jack Artenstein
Editor in Chief: Lisa Melton
Director of Publishing Services: Mary D. Aarons
Text Design: Brenda Leach/Once Upon a Design
Manufactured in the United States of America

Library of Congress Catalog Card Number: 93-42328
ISBN: 1-56565-112-X

10 9 8 7 6 5 4 3 2 1

Why Freebies??

Why do they give it away? Marketers, from companies large and small, are looking to win the battle for your dollars, and product sampling is an effective way to attract attention and make a positive impression. Studies show that allowing you to sample a company's product is more likely to result in a purchase than other marketing campaigns.

About This Book

Freebies for Fans has more than 100 offers that are sure to appeal to fans of the silver screen, television, and sports. Each offer is described as accurately as possible to help you decide which are best for you.

Unlike offers in other "get things free" books, we have confirmed with each supplier that they want you to have the offers listed in this book, and each supplier has agreed to have adequate stock on hand to honor all properly made requests.

How to Use This Book

1. Follow the Directions: Each offer specifies how to order the *freebie*. Some offers specifically request a postcard (the U.S. Post Office will not process 3 x 5 index cards in lieu of a postcard). Other offers may ask for a SASE (a long self-addressed, stamped envelope with the requested postage). If a fee is requested, include the proper amount (a check or money order is usually preferred). Use a single piece of tape to affix coins. Some suppliers may wait for out-of-town checks to clear before honoring requests.

2. Print All Information: Not everyone's handwriting is easy to read. It is always safer to neatly print your name, address, and the complete spelling of your city on your request. Be sure to include your return address on the outside of your mailing envelope or postcard. Use a ballpoint pen, typewriter, or computer to make your requests. Pencil can often smear, felt tip or ink pens easily smudge.

3. Allow Time for Your Request to Be Processed and Sent: Some suppliers send their offers via first-class mail. Others use bulk mail and this can take up to six or eight weeks. Our suppliers get thousands of requests each year and depending on the time of the year may process slower or faster than at other times.

4. What to Do if You Are Unhappy: If you are dissatisfied or have complaints about an offer, let us know. If you have not received your offer within eight to ten weeks of your request, let us know. Although we do not stock the items or offer refunds from our offices, we can follow up on your complaints with any supplier. Occasionally there are problems with a particular supplier or offer. Your letters alert us to these problems. Suppliers that generate too many complaints will not be included in future editions. Send your complaints, comments, or suggestions to:

Freebies Book Editors
1135 Eugenia Pl.
P.O. Box 5025
Carpinteria, CA 93014-5025

5. And There Is More: If you like the freebie offers you see in this book and want to see more great freebies, then you should subscribe to *Freebies* magazine. Five times a year, *Freebies* sends you a great magazine filled with approximately 100 freebies in each issue. Purchasers of *Freebies for Fans* can get a special price on a one-year/five-issue subscription of only $4.95 (the regular subscription rate is $8.95—you'll save $4.00). See the special offer on page 79.

Acknowledgments

The Freebies staff wants to say thanks to the good people at RGA/Lowell House for their support and commitment. In particular we want to acknowledge the diligent efforts of Bud Sperry, Peter Hoffman, Mary Aarons, Victoria Hsu, and Brenda Leach.

Special thanks must be accorded to Abigail Koehring and Alison Osborne for their research and writing. A thank-you is also extended to Abel Magaña, Margaret Koike, Don Weiner, Chrystal Kruse, and Angela Jacobus for their writing and editing. And, of course, thanks to Linda Cook for putting it all together.

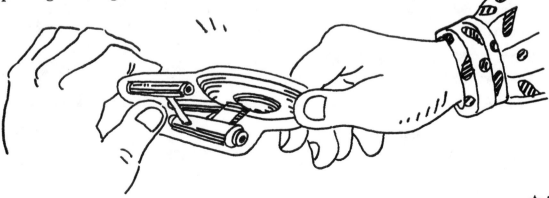

Finger Puppets
Don't Be a Stooge

☆ Wouldn't you like to bring three of the most famous funny guys into your home? Larry, Curly, and Moe will entertain you for hours on end with the **Three Stooges finger puppets**. Their rubber heads come complete with hilarious facial expressions, and each wears a ridiculous "stooge" tie and a different shirt from which flimsy hands emerge for silly swatting. Send for one or all three and be the "yuk, yuk, yuk" of your party.

Send: $3.00 for one—specify Larry, Curly, or Moe or $7.95 for all three

Ask For: The Three Stooges

Mail To: E Street Gifts
716 N. Ventura Rd., Suite 308
Oxnard, CA 93030

☆ If you love to talk about Elvis Presley, here's a fun way to start up a conversation about the King anywhere: at work, school, or even the bank. For original mementos from the Elvis Sighting Society convention, send for **five white ballpoint Presley pens**. Each one reads, "I really saw Elvis" in red lettering.

Send: $3.50 postage & handling for five

Ask For: Elvis ballpoint pens —"I really saw Elvis"

Mail To: Elvis Pens
P.O. Box 596
Summerland, CA 93067

Ballpoint Pen

Seen Elvis Lately?

☆ The art of coloring is important for children when it comes to building eye-hand coordination and color comprehension. Now you can get *The Great Fun Time Activity Book,* full of beneficial and fun-to-color pages, each book with its own classic film theme (supplier's choice). The one that we saw featured Pinocchio and included memory games, mazes, word puzzles, and much more for your child's learning entertainment.

Send: $1.50 postage & handling

Ask For: Activity book

Mail To: Sav-On
Dept. Activity Book
P.O. Box 1356
Gwinn, MI 49841

☆ It was more than two decades ago that we were first introduced to the "modern stone-age family." And we've been stuck on the Flintstones™ ever since. If you're stuck on the Flintstones too, then send for this **Flintstones sticker sheet.** Each 5" x 7" sheet consists of eight stickers featuring Fred, his family, and friends in a variety of full-color designs.

Send: $1.50 postage & handling

Ask For: Flintstones stickers

Mail To: Mr. Rainbows
Dept. FF
P.O. Box 387
Avalon, NJ 08202

STORYBOOKS

TALL TALES

☆ Remember the first time you read the story of *Jack and the Beanstalk?* Now you can help your child climb the tree of knowledge with a classic tale from the *My Tall Book* **series of children's stories** (normal retail up to $4.95). Preschool Press has designed these 5-1/2" x 11" hardcover books to exercise the mind and imagination of the preschooler. Bright, full-color illustrations with large, easy-to-read print make reading an instant fascination for any child.

Send: $2.50 postage & handling

Ask For: *My Tall Book* (various classic titles, supplier's choice)

Mail To: Sav-On
Dept. Tall Book
P.O. Box 1356
Gwinn, MI 49841

☆ If you or your friends are Johnny Carson fans, you won't be able to pass up this **commemorative key fob** honoring Johnny Carson's 30 years on "The Tonight Show." It's a collector's item made of snow-white vinyl with an inscription that reads, "The Tonight Show, 1962-1992, Starring Johnny Carson."

Send: $2.00 postage & handling for three

Ask For: Johnny Carson "The Tonight Show" key fob

Mail To: Johnny Carson key fob
P.O. Box 596
Summerland, CA 93067

Key Chain

Here's Johnny!

☆ Who's the most famous newscasting beagle in the world? The next time your dog gets the munchies, set those playful teeth into Snoopy's own newspaper, complete with real canine headlines. **Snoopy's News**, a vinyl dog bone that looks like a rolled-up newspaper ready to chew, is secured with non-toxic material and a safety squeaker—great for those "ruff" players.

Dog Bone
Squeaky Beagle

Send:	$2.50 postage & handling
Ask For:	Snoopy dog bone toy
Mail To:	Sav-On
	Dept. Snoopy News
	P.O. Box 1356
	Gwinn, MI 49841

Barbie Stickers
Doll A-Peel

☆ Barbie and her boyfriend Ken are major stars, as any little girl will tell you. Maybe it's their beaming smiles, ageless beauty, or all-American style that makes them popular. Whatever the source of their charm, you'll have lots of peel-and-stick fun with this set of **Barbie and Ken stickers**. Each card carries a different series of six 1" round stickers.

Send:	$1.25 postage & handling for one; $4.00 for set of four
Ask For:	Barbie and Ken sticker cards
Mail To:	Neetstuf
	Dept. BK
	P.O. Box 459
	Stone Harbor, NJ 08247

Star Trek® Collectibles

Tracing the Trek

☆ Attention, Trekkies! Now you can get anything from the first printings of Star Trek logs to a Star Trek sound effects key chain, featuring the sounds of the transporter, phasers, and more, with the **Star Trek collectibles catalog.** You won't want to miss this opportunity to find rare Star Trek items to add to your collection.

Send: $2.00 postage & handling

Ask For: Star Trek collectibles catalog

Mail To: Trek Co.
97 Autumn St.
Dept. B
Newport, VT 05855

☆ Celebrate Elvis Presley's trip to stardom with **a set of four Elvis pins**, each decorated with a different color photograph of the King. The set we saw included concert, candid, and posed shots. Fasten them, each about 1" in diameter, to any article of clothing or material and show off your love for one of rock 'n' roll's most influential celebrities.

Pins
Presley Pins

Send: $2.00 postage & handling for set of four

Ask For: Elvis pins—set of four

Mail To: Elvis Pins
P.O. Box 596
Summerland, CA 93067

☆ ACTION! Have you been told your kids are cute and should be in commercials? Now you can discover the secrets of how to get them started in television! *Getting Your Kids into Commercials,* a 45-minute videotape, presents interviews with top industry insiders that give you the information you need to start your child on a fun and potentially lucrative television acting career. "We are always looking for new children and new faces," says one director in the video. Could your child be that fresh new face?

Send: $9.95 postage & handling
              (regularly $19.95)

Ask For: *Getting Your Kids into Commercials*

Mail To: Mark Alyn Communications
              P.O. Box 368
              Manhattan Beach, CA 90266

MOVIE POSTER

WONDERFUL WILLY

☆ You've seen the movie; you sang along with the song; now get the promotional **poster for** *Free Willy*! The 24" x 36" full-color poster features heartwarming and breathtaking scenes from the film that will recall all the magic of the family movie.

Send: $1.00 postage & handling

Ask For: *Free Willy* poster

Mail To: Hohner Inc.
              P.O. Box 9375
              Richmond, VA 23227-5035

★ 11

Video **Star Tour**

☆ See Hollywood through the eyes of those who live and work there! *Hollywood: The Official Video Tour* takes you on a 30-minute ride down the star-studded streets of Tinseltown. Hop on the "video tour bus" and go behind-the-scenes of yesterday's Hollywood with vintage film clips and close-up looks at celebrated landmarks including the Hollywood sign and Walk of Fame. Along the way, visit with some of your favorite stars—Dick Clark, Phyllis Diller, Ed McMahon and others—as they share stories of the entertainment capital of the world.

Send: $9.95 postage & handling (regularly $19.95)

Ask For: *Hollywood: The Official Video Tour*

Mail To: Mark Alyn Communications
P.O. Box 368
Manhattan Beach, CA 90266

☆ *Learn to Be Your Own Guerilla Publicist* teaches you how to promote yourself in the entertainment world, and it's written by a man who knows the business. Receive publicity tips and techniques from author Michael Levine, one of the country's foremost publicists, who represents major celebrities, including Janet Jackson!

Publicity Pamphlet

Success Seekers

Send: A long SASE

Ask For: *Learn to Be Your Own Guerilla Publicist*

Mail To: Teach Me Guerilla P.R.
Michael Levine
8730 Sunset Blvd., 6th Floor
Los Angeles, CA 90069

☆ Cowabunga dude! The Teenage Mutant Ninja Turtles® have been framed! Catch them in their latest feature—a pair of **magnetic picture frames.**

Make your child an "Honorary Turtle" by inserting his or her photo in the frame and placing it on any metal surface (like the fridge, cool dude). You get two frames, one measuring 3" x 4-1/4" and the other 2" x 3". Both have color cartoons of the masked mugs of the Turtles along with slices of their favorite food, pizza.

Send: $2.00 postage & handling for two

Ask For: Ninja Turtle magnetic frames

Mail To: Neetstuf
              Dept. NT
              P.O. Box 459
              Stone Harbor, NJ 08247

☆ For giving or collecting, these **three assorted Christmas card records** will provide loads of entertainment. You can hear the Platters giving their version of "Jingle Bell Rock," Willie Nelson singing "Blue Christmas," and other famous recording artists belting out **classic Christmas tunes** on 45 rpm records that come in **cheerful Christmas cards.**

Send: $2.00 postage & handling for three

Ask For: Christmas card records

Mail To: Surprise Gift of the Month Club
              55 Railroad Ave.
              Garnerville, NY 10923

Batman® stickers · · · · ·
Sticky Situations

☆ Michael Keaton, Michelle Pfeiffer, and Danny DeVito, a.k.a. Batman®, Catwoman®, and the Penguin®, can now belong to you! With this offer you receive **three cards of *Batman Returns* removable stickers.** Each of the three cards features eight different action poses of popular Batman characters just as you saw them in the movie!

Send: $2.00 postage & handling for three cards
Ask For: *Batman Returns* stickers
Mail To: Mr. Rainbows
Dept. BR
P.O. Box 387
Avalon, NJ 08202

☆ They're stars just for kids! Award-winning recording artists Joanie Bartels, Dennis Hysome, and Bethie sing fun, silly songs especially for children. Receive *The Stars of Discovery Music*, a special, full-length **audio cassette** at reduced cost (regular retail price is $9.98), full of great kids' music by great performers. You'll also get a **free catalog!**

Audio Cassette
Discovery Stars

Send: $2.00 postage & handling
Ask For: *The Stars of Discovery Music*
Mail To: Discovery Music
5554 Calhoun Ave.
Van Nuys, CA 91401

☆ Add an **authentic reproduction of the 1-ELVIS Tennessee State license plate** to your Hollywood collection.

Made of metal in the state colors of red, white, and blue and measuring 11-7/8" x 6", this full-size license plate is a great conversation piece. Whether it's displayed on your car or wall, everyone will surely ask, "Where did you find that?" Just tell them the King gave it to you.

Send:	$5.95 postage & handling
Ask For:	Elvis license plate
Mail To:	MailAway USA 635 N. Milpas St., Dept. W Santa Barbara, CA 93103

☆ Let your child experience the magic of classic fairy tales such as Snow White and the Seven Dwarfs, Sleeping Beauty, Cinderella, Aladdin, and others with a **full-size coloring book.**

The book features more than 60 fun and memorable scenes from beloved tales and is guaranteed to provide hours of coloring entertainment. Supplier's choice of story title.

Send:	$1.50 postage & handling
Ask For:	Coloring book
Mail To:	Sav-On Dept. Coloring Book P.O. Box 1356 Gwinn, MI 49841

Lapel Pin

☆ Felix fans! Before Garfield or Morris there was Felix! So don't miss this **Felix the Cat lapel pin** featuring the famous feline. Attach the 2" soft rubber figure wherever you'd like and let Felix's happy grin remind you of his mischievous ways—and all the fun you had watching him get into and out of trouble.

Send:	$1.75 postage & handling
Ask For:	Felix lapel pin
Mail To:	E Street Gifts
	716 N. Ventura Rd., Suite 308
	Oxnard, CA 93030

☆ You've seen them on the big screen; you've seen them on TV; now you can see them wherever you stick them. Here come the **Teenage Mutant Ninja Turtles®** again! Act now and receive **16 stickers** of eight different designs featuring your favorite pizza-eating heroes on the half shell.

Send:	$1.50 postage & handling
Ask For:	Teenage Mutant Ninja Turtle stickers
Mail To:	Mr. Rainbows
	Dept. MNT
	P.O. Box 387
	Avalon, NJ 08202

☆ Everyone's making it big, and Nintendo video characters are no exception. And now you can collect **16 stickers featuring** the ever-popular **Mario Brothers** in action. You'll get two different 5" x 7" sheets of stickers with the nifty brothers in colorful action shots on a silver backing.

Nintendo Stickers
Mad About Mario

Send: $2.00 postage & handling for two sheets

Ask For: Nintendo stickers

Mail To: Neetstuf
Dept. MB
P.O. Box 459
Stone Harbor, NJ 08247

Rubber Stamper
Stamp Paddington

☆ Paddington Bear™ has warmed children's hearts for years. He's appeared in wonderful stories and now appears on a unique **rolling stamper.** Standing 2-1/2" tall, the rolling wheel ($4.95 retail in stores) creates four cute impressions: Paddington's darling face, a "FRAGILE" label, Paddington's paw prints, and a luggage tag that reads, "Please look after this bear. Thank you."

Send: $1.75 postage & handling

Ask For: Paddington Bear stamper

Mail To: E Street Gifts
716 N. Ventura Rd., Suite 308
Oxnard, CA 93030

Magnet

Be Enterprising

☆ Boldly go where no one has gone before with a **Star Trek® U.S.S. *Enterprise*® magnet.**

Approximately 4" in length, this soft rubber magnet replica of the U.S.S. *Enterprise* will easily hold your most important messages from this galaxy or the next—proving there's no starship better than the *Enterprise*.

Send:	$1.75 postage & handling
Ask For:	Star Trek Enterprise magnet
Mail To:	Esther's E-Z Shop P.O. Box 1831 Pomona, CA 91769 Attn: SEM

☆ Be the first on your block with **"Screamin' Traders" horror movie trading cards.** Receive three cards featuring still shots and information from your favorite horror flicks.

Just think, you can "possess" a card with *Friday the 13th*'s Jason, posed with ax in hand, in your Hollywood horror classic collection!

TRADING CARDS

HORRIFIC HOLLYWOOD

Send:	A long SASE
Ask For:	Screamin' Traders sample pack
Mail To:	Cinema & Celebrities P.O. Box 4815 Cave Creek, AZ 85331

☆ Here's a great find for collectors and fans. Save on this **catalog** ($3.00 cover price) **of 8" x 10" movie, television, and music performer books and photos**—past and present. The 116 pages provide photos of stars and a listing of more than 2,000 pictures. You'll find photos you never dreamed you could have, and a large selection of movie books to inform you about your favorite films and stars.

Photo Catalog

𝒫hond of Photos

Send: $2.00 postage & handling

Ask For: *Movie Star Books & Photos*

Mail To: Empire Publishing
Box 717
Madison, NC 27025-0717

Fan Newsletter
Mayberry Memories

☆ Yearning for the simple times and friendly smiles of Mayberry, USA? Then act now and receive a sample issue of *The Bullet*—the official newsletter of "The Andy Griffith Show" Rerun Watchers Club (TAGSRWC).

Now you can keep up with Opie and Barney and upcoming events of TAGSRWC and relive your favorite Mayberry memories.

Send: A long SASE with two first-class stamps affixed

Ask For: *The Bullet*

Mail To: TAGSRWC
42 Music Square West, Suite 146
Nashville, TN 37203-3234

Beatles Magazine

Getting Beatles All the Time

☆ Beatlemania is still alive and kicking, so to all you Beatlemaniacs out there—this one's for you! Receive a **sample of the current edition of** *Good Day Sunshine* and pay less.

The magazine, which retails for $3.00, is full of interviews and photos, keeping you in close contact with the fab four, past and present.

Send: $2.00 postage & handling

Ask For: Sample magazine

Mail To: Good Day Sunshine
c/o Charles F. Rosenay III
397 Edgewood Ave.
New Haven, CT 06511

☆ The latest trend in collectibles are old-fashioned water decals. Start with this set of five assorted **vintage decals** that you dip in water and slide on any flat surface to stick. The selection we saw included Alfred E. Newman, the trademark character of *Mad* magazine, a U.S. flag, flags and pennants from various states and sports teams, "The South Will Rise Again" bumper sticker, and an "Official U.S. Taxpayer" decal.

Send: $1.00 postage & handling

Ask For: Five decals

Mail To: Parker Flags and Pennants
5746 Plunkett St., Suite 4
Hollywood, FL 33023-2346

DECALS

DECAL COLLECTING

☆ FAN-atical collectors! Don't miss this opportunity to receive a copy of *Autograph Collector* magazine—normal retail is $4.95—at a bargain price!

Learn how to write to your favorite stars and receive free celebrity signatures to start or add to your autograph collection. Plus, find opportunities to buy rare autographs or sell yours for top dollar!

Send: $2.00 postage & handling

Ask For: *Autograph Collector* magazine

Mail To: Autograph Collector
510-A S. Corona Mall
Corona, CA 91720

☆ Never before have you been able to find so many listings for film and television collectibles. This **sample of *Big Reel***, offered here for less than its $3.00 cover price, provides a huge, tabloid-size publication—more than 100 pages—full of old, rare, and new collector's items. You'll be dazzled by the videos, posters, photos, books, and other items available to you.

Send: $1.00 postage & handling

Ask For: Sample of "Big Reel"

Mail To: Empire Publishing
Box 717
Madison, NC 27025-0717

☆ The Hollywood sun has been great for the California Dancing Raisins, and now these cute and cheerful characters can spread some sunshine your way while keeping track of your keys. You'll always have a star in the palm of your hand with your 2" **California Raisin key chain,** which comes in one of four adorable poses.

Send: $1.75 postage & handling

Ask For: California Raisin key chain

Mail To: Tom Schmeelk
18 Durland Pl.
Brooklyn, NY 11236

☆ He looks like celebrity Dom DeLuise, but his cooking, not his comedy, caused his rise to fame. And now, Chef Paul Prudhomme, famous New Orleans restaurateur, would like to share his talents with you.

Receive **two trial-size packets** of his new **Magic Pepper Sauce, a 40¢ coupon, and a K-Paul's Louisiana mail order catalog,** which includes five recipes from Chef Paul.

Send: $1.00 postage & handling

Ask For: Chef Paul pack

Mail To: Magic Seasoning Blends
P.O. Box 23342
New Orleans, LA 70183-0342

☆ Expose your children to theater at an early age with the **Children's Theatre cassette** featuring the charming and classic tales of *Pinocchio* and *Jack and the Beanstalk.* Each side of the cassette runs about 20 minutes with actors presenting the stories in theatrical style, and they're accompanied by a live orchestra!

TAPED TALENT

Send: $2.00 postage & handling

Ask For: Children's Theatre cassette

Mail To: R.H. Bauman
9258 Deering Ave.
Chatsworth, CA 91311

Celebrity Addresses

Word to the Stars

☆ Now you can write to your favorite celebrities! Michael Levine has spent much time and effort finding the mailing addresses of famous people, and now he's willing to share them with you for free!

With this fun offer you receive **20 addresses of superstars** from pop stars to politicians—for free!

Send: A long SASE

Ask For: 20 superstar mailing addresses

Mail To: Michael Levine
The Address Book
8730 Sunset Blvd., 6th Floor
Los Angeles, CA 90069

☆ The cartoon characters of Walt Disney have become big, big celebrities, and this collection of **50 Disney stamps** proves it! The genuine Disney postage stamps are all different and feature your favorite Disney stars in all kinds of fun, worldly situations. You'll also receive a **collector stamp catalog** so your collection can grow as big as these stars. Plus, you'll receive stamps on approval to buy if you like and return the balance—but the Disney stamps are yours free.

Send: $1.00 postage & handling

Ask For: Disney stamps and catalog

Mail To: Jamestown Stamp Co.
341-3 East 3rd
Jamestown, NY 14701-0019

☆ Pennants and hats may show support for your favorite sports team, but now you can really express yourself with this set of realistic **temporary tattoos**. They are safe, non-toxic, easy to apply, and easy to remove. Each package of two tattoos (one large and one small) normally retails for $3.99 or more, but you can save 25% with this special offer.

Send: $3.00 postage & handling

Ask For: The specific team and sport you want

Mail To: World of Tattoos
Box 304
Allenhurst, NJ 07711

☆ Imagine a video catalog that features classic and not-so-classic westerns, serials, war documentaries, horror and science fiction films, cartoons, and foreign films! Now...there's a **free video catalog** with all this and more! Just ask for it and find every video you've ever wanted.

Send: Your name & address

Ask For: Free video catalog

Mail To: Discount Video Tapes, Inc.
P.O. Box 7122
Burbank, CA 91510

☆ If you're still stuck on "Gilligan's Island" here's your chance to reminisce with your favorite stranded castaways. You can receive **information about the Original Gilligan's Island Fan Club,** which will give you the opportunity to receive a fan-club T-shirt, photos of the castaways, newsletters, and much more.

Send: A long SASE

Ask For: Fan club information

Mail To: The Original Gilligan's Island Fan Club
P.O. Box 25311
Salt Lake City, UT 84125-0311
Attn: Bob

Tattoos

Beam Me Up, Freddy

☆ It's Friday the 13th, you're on Elm Street, and you must be careful of who, or what, is lurking out there. Is it Star Trek, Jurassic dinosaurs, monsters from Universal Studios, Jason of *Friday the 13th* fame, or Freddy Krueger fresh from *A Nightmare on Elm Street?* The choice is yours when you order a set of these safe, non-toxic **temporary tattoos**. Each package has at least two (sorry, but Star Trek has only one tattoo) detailed, full-color tattoos.

Send: $3.00 postage & handling
Ask For: Specify which set you want
Mail To: World of Tattoos
Box 304
Allenhurst, NJ 07711

☆ Finding celebrity memorabilia for your movie, TV, music, and theater collections can be frustrating. But with a sample issue of the quarterly publication *Celebrity Collector*, you should have no problem finding the right stars. Offered now for only $2.00 (that's more than 50% off its cover price of $5.00), this 20-page magazine, created to serve as a network for collectors around the world, includes interviews, classifieds, and much more.

Collector's Publication

A Collector's Connection

Send: $2.00 postage & handling
Ask For: *Celebrity Collector* sample issue
Mail To: Celebrity Collector
P.O. Box 1115
Boston, MA 02117

☆ Gain instant celebrity status with **three Notable Marquee personalized note cards.** The 4" x 5-1/2" cards feature a black imprint of a Gothic theater exterior and a movie marquee carrying the words "HOLLYWOOD" and "The [Your Name] Story," proving to all that you're worthy of notice.

Send: $2.50 postage & handling for three cards and envelopes

Ask For: Notable Marquee Note Cards. Specify the first and last name to be printed on the cards. Please print clearly.

Mail To: Parallel Universe Enterprises
2210 Wilshire Blvd., Suite 757
Santa Monica, CA 90403

Limit: One set per address

Movie Magazines

B last from the Past

☆ Have you ever wished for a copy of an old movie magazine, just to remember what it was like, say, when *Star Wars* first appeared on the big screen? Well, now it's possible with **three assorted old movie magazines** that'll blast you right back into the filmmaking past! And they're great collector's items.

Send: $2.00 postage & handling for three

Ask For: Old movie magazines

Mail To: Surprise Gift of the Month Club
55 Railroad Ave.
Garnerville, NY 10923

Book

He's Magic

☆ An inspiring biography about one of the most unforgettable people of our time, *The Magic Man* is an 80-page in-depth look at Earvin "Magic" Johnson. With a retail price of $3.95, *Freebies* readers will save nearly $2.00 for this special book, complete with black-and-white photographs.

Send: $2.00 postage & handling

Ask For: *The Magic Man* book

Mail To: RGA Publishing Group, Inc.
2029 Century Park East, Suite 3290
Los Angeles, CA 90067
Attn: Dept. VH

☆ If you enjoy watching the popular ABC soap opera **"One Life to Live,"** you'll love this opportunity. Get to know Karen Witter ("Tina Lord Roberts") or Laura Bonarrigo ("Cassie Callison Carpenter") by applying for **fan club membership** or receiving a **sample newsletter** full of interesting information and photos!

Fan Club

Fun Life to Live

Send: Your name & address & a loose first-class stamp for membership application OR $2.00 postage & handling for sample newsletter

Ask For: Membership application OR newsletter—specify Karen or Laura

Mail To: Funky Fan Clubs
P.O. Box 9624
New Haven, CT 06535

☆ Thanks to the magic of video, Elvis Presley can come to life on screen at your request. Complete with order form and a listing of more than 40 Elvis movies, music, and memories available for purchase, **The Elvis Video List** will give you plenty of opportunity to reminisce about the King.

Send: One first-class stamp

Ask For: Elvis video list and order form

Mail To: From This Old House
Box 468-F
Almont, MI 48003

☆ Who are your favorite stars . . . really? With *What Did You Say Your Name Was?*, a **booklet containing more than 200 stars' names,** you'll find out (and sometimes poke fun at) the original names of your favorite famous people. Satisfy your curiosity by sending for this fun booklet today!

Send: $1.00 postage & handling

Ask For: Names booklet

Mail To: S & H Trading Co.
1187 Coast Village #208
Montecito, CA 93108-2794

Collector Catalog
Oz-some

☆ Every man, woman, and child remembers *The Wizard of Oz*, and with a **sample of *The Oz Collector***, those memories can become even more special. You'll get an illustrated catalog of everything Oz, including the books by Baum and illustrations by Denslow that began this fairy tale in 1900, as well as other Oz-some memorabilia.

Send: $2.00 postage & handling

Ask For: *The Oz Collector*

Mail To: The Oz Collector
P.O. Box 714, Box FR
New York, NY 10011

☆ Do you adore those little blue cartoon creatures known all over the world as the Smurfs? Well, you'll be delighted by this opportunity to receive **information about the Smurf Collector's Club International**.

The club provides listings of rare collector's items, including European collectibles that are usually not available in the USA. Get your information today!

Collector's Club
Simply Smurfy

Send: A long SASE

Ask For: Club membership information

Mail To: Smurf Collector's Club International
24 Cabot Rd. West
Dept. Kids
Massapequa, NY 11758

☆ Attention, soap opera fans: Your devotion to soaps has finally paid off! Now you are eligible for a wonderful and useful offer. A **12" ruler imprinted with "I LOVE THE SOAPS"** expresses your immeasurable appreciation for daytime drama. Don't delay!

Send:	$2.00 postage & handling
Ask For:	"I LOVE THE SOAPS" ruler
Mail To:	Carol Dickson
	1218 N. Main St.
	Glassboro, NJ 08028

☆ Want to make it big as a songwriter? Then check out an **issue of** *Songwriter's Monthly*. It's full of helpful information about the music industry and is loaded with interviews and songwriting tips to provide a support system for struggling artists. It just might give you the encouragement you need to succeed!

Send:	$1.00 postage & handling
Ask For:	*Songwriter's Monthly*
Mail To:	Songwriter's Monthly
	332 Eastwood Ave.
	Feasterville, PA 19053

Star Trek®
Bookmark
Hollywood Hologram

☆ Show your devotion to the epic "Star Trek®" series with this stellar **Star Trek® hologram bookmark**. The 6" x 2" bookmark features three scenes from either "Star Trek®" or "Star Trek: The Next Generation®". The amazing hologram images come alive right in your hands!

Send:	$2.25 postage & handling
Ask For:	*Star Trek* hologram bookmark
Mail To:	Esther's E-Z Shop P.O. Box 1831-SB Pomona, CA 91769

☆ It's your turn to make a movie with the **Take One acrylic frame**. The 1-7/8" x 1-1/4" photo holder looks like a mini movie-set clapboard that holds your favorite picture! Just choose whether you'd like a key chain or a magnetic frame.

Send:	$2.00 postage & handling
Ask For:	Take One: specify key chain or magnetic memo holder
Mail To:	The Complete Traveler 490 Rte. 46 East Fairfield, NJ 07004

☆ Everyone knows it's tough to make it in Hollywood, so here's an offer that might make things a little easier. You can receive a complete **list of more than 400 Screen Actors Guild franchised talent agencies** in the entire country, all the way from Hollywood to New York! Then, contact the agencies of your choice, and go for it!

Send: $1.95 postage & handling

Ask For: List of talent agents

Mail To: Kelly Farrell
309 Ruby St.
Redondo Beach, CA 90277

☆ Find fun and fascinating pieces of movie, television, and rock 'n' roll memorabilia in the **TV Collector Memorabilia and Collectibles catalog.** In addition to the listing of old gossip magazines, you can find such items as a 1976 "Welcome Back, Kotter" card game, an LP of Steve Martin's "A Wild and Crazy Guy," even a 1943 *Brenda Starr, Girl Reporter* adventure book.

Send: $1.95 postage & handling

Ask For: *TV Collector* catalog

Mail To: The TV Collector
P.O. Box 1088-C
Easton, MA 02334

Classic TV

Those Were the Days

☆ Now you can experience—again—showbiz as it was in the '50s and '60s with **TV's Magic Memories video catalog**. It features listings of available videos of classic television shows and movies, some with their original commercials! With the catalog you'll also receive a **coupon for free shipping of your first order** ($4 value).

Send: $1.00 postage & handling
Ask For: TV's Magic Memories video catalog
Mail To: Moviecraft, Inc.
Dept. FRB
P.O. Box 438
Orland Park, IL 60462

☆ Find your favorite western and serial stars in this **free sample issue of *Westerns and Serials***, featuring photos galore of classic actors like John Wayne, Roy Rogers, and many more! You'll read interesting articles, learn where your favorite movies are showing today, and find a catalog section of memorabilia information. Please note that due to the nature of this free offer and the costs involved in production and mailing of the offer, this supplier mails only four times during the year. Please be patient.

Fan Magazine

Way Back Westerns

Send: Your name & address
Ask For: *Westerns and Serials* sample
Mail To: Norman Kietzer
Rte. 1, Box 103
Vernon Center, MN 56090

☆ Who's your hero? Thanks to John Blumenthal Autographs, here's your chance to take home a statement, paper, or picture signed by your favorite person's very own hand. Send for this **autograph catalog**, featuring autographs for sale from presidents, astronauts, movie stars, musicians, authors, scientists, and more, and place your very own special order.

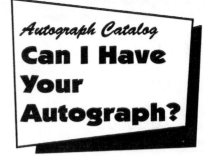

Send: $1.00 postage & handling

Ask For: Autograph catalog

Mail To: John Blumenthal Autographs
5123 Belaire Ave.
North Hollywood, CA 91607

☆ If you're not looking to the most celebrated canine for holiday gift ideas, you're barking up the wrong tree. Snoopy senses when Santa is on his way and has conveniently sniffed out a foot-long **holiday stocking**, featuring himself and his bird buddy, Woodstock, singing on a sleigh—a great gift idea for everyone from young adults to toddlers to pets.

Send: $2.00 postage & handling

Ask For: Snoopy Christmas stocking

Mail To: Sav-On
Dept. Snoopy stocking
P.O. Box 1356
Gwinn, MI 49841

SOMETHING FOR NOTHING

☆ Can you use fun items such as holiday craft projects, safety scissors, rulers, stickers, fun pencils, novelty erasers, bookmarks, and more? Are you a fan of educational items such as *Science Weekly*, museum guides, nutrition charts, whale activity kits, maps and more??

Then you need *Freebies* **magazine**. Each issue features approximately 100 useful, informative, and fun items that are available for free or for a small postage and handling cost.

Send: $2.00 postage & handling for one sample issue or $4.95 for a one-year, five-issue subscription (regular rate is $8.95)

Ask For: Sample issue of *Freebies* or a one-year subscription as indicated above.

Mail To: Freebies/Fans Offer
1135 Eugenia Pl.
P.O. Box 5025
Carpinteria, CA 93014-5025

☆ Get 12 holes in one when you send for this 12-piece Putt-Putt™ golf **jigsaw puzzle**. This is a great first jigsaw puzzle for youngsters. When finished, it shows a happy golfer, an alligator, elephant, giraffe, and zebra on the golf course.

Jigsaw Puzzle

Hole in One

Send: $1.80 postage & handling

Ask For: Jigsaw puzzle

Mail To: Putt-Putt Golf Freebies Offer
Box 35237
Fayetteville, NC 28303

☆ Would you like to be inspired by a photograph of your favorite celeb? Or by an autograph? **The Celebrity Photo catalog** lists hundreds of available quality photos, in black and white and color, including both studio and candid shots of celebrities. Also listed are celebrity autographs, posters, color slides, and more, accompanied by product prices and an order form.

Send: $2.00 postage & handling

Ask For: Celebrity Photo catalog

Mail To: California Hot Shots
P.O. Box 3122
San Leandro, CA 94578

☆ Many people have tried it, loved it, and brought it to fame, and now you can bring it into your own kitchen. Cut a slice of salad history for yourself with the **authentic Cobb Salad recipe**, straight from the collection of the late president of the original landmark Hollywood Brown Derby Restaurant, Mr. Robert H. Cobb. Surely this could be the key to some of your tastiest meals.

Send: $1.00 postage & handling

Ask For: Recipe for Cobb Salad at the Brown Derby Restaurant

Mail To: Mary Moore
18715 Kross Rd.
Riverside, CA 92508

Shady Photos

☆ A limited supply of rare 8" x 10" photographs of your favorite characters from America's scariest gothic soap opera, "Dark Shadows," is available along with the opportunity to become a member of the "Dark Shadows" fan club. You will receive one **8" x 10" photograph** from a collection of nine different portraits (supplier's choice).

Send:	$2.00 postage & handling plus a 9" x 12" SASE with two first-class stamps affixed
Ask For:	Dark Shadows 8" x 10" photograph
Mail To:	The Dark Shadows Fan Club
	Dept. DSFG
	P.O. Box 69A04
	West Hollywood, CA 90069

☆ Add some of Walt Disney's imaginative characters to your address labels. Send for a **set of 24 address labels**, printed with your own name and address, and stamped with your choice of a classic Disney face. You can also order your personally addressed labels plain, for your own decorating ideas.

The Faces of Disney

Send:	$1.50 postage & handling for the set of 24
Ask For:	Personalized Disney address labels. Specify Mickey, Minnie, Goofy, or Donald Duck.
Mail To:	His 'N Hers
	P.O. Box 5902
	Knoxville, TN 37928

☆ Everybody recognizes the beautiful faces of Cindy Crawford, Naomi Campbell, Niki Taylor, and Claudia Schiffer, but who are the people behind the faces? With a hip, magazine-style design and tons of candid photos, *Supermodels* is a 32-page book delivering stories, stats, quotes, and health tips from 15 of the world's most famous superstar models. With a retail price of $2.95, *Supermodels* is now being offered to *Freebies* readers for $1.75, providing over $1.00 savings for this super-fascinating info.

Send: $1.75 postage & handling

Ask For: *Supermodels* book

Mail To: RGA Publishing Group, Inc.
2029 Century Park East, Suite 3290
Los Angeles, CA 90067
Attn: Dept. VH

☆ Few people know there's a Klingon dictionary on the market, but even fewer know that there are two Klingon alphabets! The **Klingon Assault Group** is a Star Trek® fan organization. There are no dues, and growth is based on communication and cooperation. If you want to be a member of a scout ship, send for the membership form and you will receive a sample of their latest newsletter.

Send: A long SASE

Ask For: Klingon Assault Group information

Mail To: KRIS/KAG Command, John Halvorson
P.O. Box 421
Reese, MI 48757

Autograph
Information
*Star
Contact*

☆ Now, thanks to Jim Weaver and his amazing **celebrity autograph address lists,** you can possess the autograph you've always dreamed about.

The lists feature movie stars, singers, and glamour symbols who willingly send their photos and autographs to adoring fans. Contact him, and he'll help you contact the stars.

Send: Your name and address

Ask For: Address list information

Mail To: Jim Weaver
405 Dunbar Dr.
Pittsburgh, PA 15235

☆ If you can't beat 'em (or meet 'em), you can laugh at 'em in the *Hollywood Cartoon Parade,* a 20-page, black-and-white booklet filled with "what-if" cartoons and outrageous one-liners you would never hear off the set. It's showbiz behind the scenes . . . totally made up to make you laugh.

Send: $2.00 postage & handling

Ask For: *Hollywood Cartoon Parade* book

Mail To: Bowman Publishing
743 Harvard Ave.
St. Louis, MO 63130-3135

Cartoons
That's Showbiz

☆ Keep classic celebs close to you with a **Hollywood key chain.** On one side of this 2 1/2", clear, solid plastic decoration is the Hollywood sign with a strip of film in the background, and on the other side are classic black-and-white pictures of Elizabeth Taylor, John Wayne, and Marilyn Monroe.

Send: $1.50 for one or $2.50 for two

Ask For: Hollywood key chain

Mail To: S & H Trading Co.
1187 Coast Village #208
Montecito, CA 93108-2794

☆ If you want to show off your favorite sports player, snap it with a **Lockermate.** Pick your **single** favorite sportscard, snap it into this clear **acrylic** frame, and hang it on lockers, refrigerators, etc., **by** its supportive magnetic backstrip. With **this** magnetic mini snaptite, your card will be on **display** and totally protected. With this great offer you'll receive the holder and a sports card with **your** choice of sport.

Send: $1.00 postage & handling

Ask For: Lockermate, and specify baseball, hockey, football, or basketball

Mail To: The 10th Inning
P.O. Box 5902
Knoxville, TN 37928

TIME TO DECORATE

☆ Shop where the stars shop! If you want to add some character to your cute stuff, put in your $2.00 request for a **miniature Gucci shopping bag** (normally $5.75 retail) and also receive a four-page **miniatures brochure** dealing in dollhouse furnishings, complete with photographs and order form.

Send: $2.00 postage & handling

Ask For: Miniature Gucci shopping bag and miniatures brochure

Mail To: Markham Studios
Dept. 808
461 Lynbrook Dr.
Pacifica, CA 94044

☆ America's funniest family of fright has come to haunt you in five collectible Munster family postcards. Along with an application for the Munsters and the Addams Family fan club, the supplier will select for you a very special **Munster postcard.** He will choose from his stock of five different photographs, each portraying an individual member of this funky family, or one portraying the Munster family together in their TV home.

Munster
Postcards

*M*unster
Madness

Send: $1.00 postage & handling plus a long SASE

Ask For: Munsters postcard

Mail To: The Munsters Fan Club
Dept. MPC
P.O. Box 69A04
West Hollywood, CA 90069

☆ There are classics in movies, TV, and books, and there are definitely classics in rock music. Offered to you by *Brain Damage* magazine are a variety of funky 8-1/2" x 11" **Pink Floyd mini posters** (selected by the supplier). Prints we saw portrayed classic Pink Floyd concert announcements, including the Love-In Festival '67, the Bank in Los Angeles '68, Tour '72, Dane County Coliseum '73, and last but not least, The Wall Tour '80.

Mini Posters
Floyd Fever

Send:	$1.00 postage & handling
Ask For:	Pink Floyd mini poster
Mail To:	*Brain Damage* magazine P.O. Box 109 Westmont, IL 60559

Soap Opera Star Bios

Behind the Scenes

☆ It's easy to get tied up in the lives of daytime TV characters, but have you considered the personalities behind the pictures? Directly from *The Soap Opera Book: Who's Who in Daytime Drama,* you can receive **five sample biographies** of soap opera actors and actresses of your choice, along with a copy of **fan club lists.**

Send:	$2.00 postage & handling
Ask For:	Bios of your five favorite soap stars
Mail To:	Todd Publications 18 N. Greenbush Rd. West Nyack, NY 10994

☆ If you're tired of ordinary sports posters, it's time to check out hot new illustrations of your idols, drawn by the top sports artists of today, in the **Celebrity Prints catalog.** Pictures advertised—colored, autographed (by artist, subject, or both), and ready to frame—famous sports players in action like Troy Aikman, Larry Bird, and Dan Marino, an "after the game" theme with Joe Montana's jersey and helmet, and paraphernalia from Nolan Ryan.

Send: $2.00 postage & handling

Ask For: Celebrity limited edition prints catalog

Mail To: Celebrity Publishing Group
P.O. Box 1986
South Hackensack, NJ 07606

☆ You can do your part to help save the planet by learning about various recycling methods. Send for the Putt-Putt™ Golf Buster Ball **coloring book** and learn about saving energy and the environment as you color the pictures. Follow Buster Ball from the backyard to the garage to the recycling center and help color your world green.

Coloring Book
Color It Green

Send: $1.25 postage & handling

Ask For: Recycling coloring book

Mail To: Putt-Putt Golf Freebies Offer
Box 35237
Fayetteville, NC 28303

☆ Stamp your favorite star's name with a ready-to-use, sturdily **mounted rubber stamp**. On one line of a sheet of lined paper, clearly print desired names such as Kevin Costner, Madonna, Clint Eastwood, or anything else you can imagine. Limit each line to 20 characters or less, and make sure to include your full name and address at the bottom of the paper.

Send: $1.00 postage & handling

Ask For: Rubber stamp with favorite star's name

Mail To: Ramastamps
Dept. FH
7924 Soper Hill Rd.
Everett, WA 98205

☆ There's nothing that warms your heart more than a movie, except maybe a movie soundtrack. **Soundtracks Original Cast Albums catalog** provides a thorough listing of original soundtracks compiled by people who have been in the business of selling collectible recordings for 21 years and can provide rarities that are unavailable anywhere else.

Send: $1.00 postage & handling

Ask For: Soundtracks Original Cast Albums catalog

Mail To: RTS
Dept. FB
P.O. Box 93897
Las Vegas, NV 89193-3897

Sportscard Holder
Stand Up

☆ For an original way to display your sports hero, make a dive for the **Top Load display stand,** which allows you to showcase your best sportscard in a protective acrylic case for all the world to see. Send for your display stand and receive this protective case, plus a complimentary sportscard with your choice of sport: baseball, football, basketball, or hockey.

Send: $1.00 postage & handling

Ask For: Top Load display stand with one sportscard (specify sport)

Mail To: The 10th Inning
P.O. Box 5902
Knoxville, TN 37928

☆ Add charm to your attire with this sparkling accessory. Made of sterling silver, this dainty little **charm** reads "A Star Is Born" and is an especially glamorous complement to silver bracelet and necklace chains. Cute yet elegant, this charm will give you the confidence of a star. You can also order a matching 7" sterling silver bracelet to accompany the charm.

Charm
*T*winkle, Twinkle

Send: $1.95 postage & handling for either the charm or the bracelet

Ask For: Sterling silver "Star Is Born" charm, and/or bracelet

Mail To: Two Gals with the Gift
P.O. Box 747
Forestville, CA 95436

☆ Hollywood's greatest comedy trio, The Three Stooges, come to life in the **Soitenly Stooges memorabilia catalog**. With a variety of officially licensed offers for T-shirts, videos, watches, posters, ties, books, and much more, you're sure to "n'yuk" it up and find some truly unique products for your collection or enjoyment.

Send:	$2.00 postage & handling
Ask For:	Soitenly Stooges memorabilia catalog
Mail To:	Soitenly Stooges Inc. P.O. Box 72 Skokie, IL 60076

☆ Collect a beautiful (and classy!) **postcard of Diana Ross and the Supremes** from the Girl Groups fan club and receive an opportunity to become a fan club member. The supplier will choose between a color close-up of the three Supremes and a classic black-and-white full body shot of one of the members.

Send:	$1.00 postage & handling plus a long SASE
Ask For:	Supremes postcard
Mail To:	Dept. SPC The Girl Groups Fan Club P.O. Box 69A04 West Hollywood, CA 90069

Information Packet

Six of One

☆ In 1977 the Prisoner Appreciation Society was formed to celebrate the classic 17-part late-1960s British TV series, "The Prisoner." Now you can send for an **information packet** revealing answers to the questions most often asked about the fun and fascinating series, as well as instructions on how to become a member of this 16-year organization.

Send: A long SASE

Ask For: "The Prisoner" newsletter—British TV series

Mail To: The Prisoner Appreciation Society
871 Clover Dr.
North Wales, PA 19454

☆ Grab hold of this giant pen with both hands to help you with your homework and letters. This Putt-Putt™ Golf **giant pen** is over 6" tall and over 1-1/2" round and features the still popular happy face. The point is retractable, so there's no mess in your pocket or notebook.

Giant Pen

Write Well

Send: $1.50 postage & handling and a long SASE

Ask For: Giant pen

Mail To: Putt-Putt Golf Freebies Offer
Box 35237
Fayetteville, NC 28303

☆ Searching through a video store (or many) for a favorite movie can be frustrating, so why not video shop from your own home? Now, simply by flipping through the pages of this **video catalog,** you will have access to a large variety of movies, including some rare video collectibles. It's the perfect way to expand your collection . . . without the frustration.

Send: $1.00 postage & handling

Ask For: Video movie catalog

Mail To: RTS
Dept. FB
P.O. Box 93897
Las Vegas, NV 89193-3897

☆ Where does your day stand in entertainment history? Mail in the name and date of a baby's birthday, your birthday, a wedding anniversary, or a general day of interest, and you will receive a **personalized report** on 8-1/2" x 11" parchment with graphic borders and a list of famous events that have taken place on the same day in previous years.

Send: $6.00 for three different reports (minimum order)

Ask For: Your Day in History—personalized by date and name

Mail To: Ocotillo Hills Press
P.O. Box 9734-H
Phoenix, AZ 85020

Television Magazine **Memory Lane**

☆ TV buffs will love this offer! A **sample issue of** *The TV Collector*, which normally sells for $3.00, will delight and surprise you. The magazine provides in-depth information, interviews, and fascinating facts. It brings back vivid memories of the classics and even tells you where you can find them on your TV!

Send: $2.00 postage & handling

Ask For: *TV Collector* magazine—mention *Freebies*

Mail To: The TV Collector
P.O. Box 1088-M
Easton, MA 02334

☆ In this sport, the more strikes the merrier. Bowling is a game of getting strikes and recording your score for all to see, and the National Bowling Hall of Fame and Museum wants to make it easier for you with this **commemorative pencil and sticker** that features its logo. This is one time you'll want to stay in the alley!

Pencil and Sticker

Striking Out!

Send: 50¢ and a long SASE

Ask For: Pencil and sticker

Mail To: National Bowling Hall of Fame
111 Stadium Plaza
St. Louis, MO 63102

☆ Alive and dead are words you will need to know as you move through the course and get set to hit the finishing stake. What course?? What game?? You'll find out when you send for the **instructional pamphlet and button** for the game of croquet. It's a sport for the entire family that can be played almost anywhere. The pamphlet gives you rules, strategy, and other information on this fun game.

ALIVE, DEAD, AND CROQUET

Send: 52¢ postage & handling

Ask For: *Croquet Is OK* pamphlet and button

Mail To: USCA
500 Avenue of the Champions
Palm Beach Gardens, FL 33418

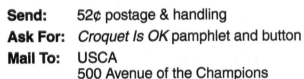

Game
Fore!

☆ You don't need good weather or expensive equipment to play golf—just a pencil is all you need when you send for the **Putt-Putt™ pencil golf course**. Your tee time is guaranteed when you play this simulated nine-hole placemat-size course that tests your accuracy as you go from hole to hole and tests your math skills as you add your "strokes."

Send: $1.00 & a long SASE

Ask For: Pencil Putt-Putt golf course

Mail To: Putt-Putt Golf Freebies Offer
Box 35237
Fayetteville, NC 28303

Tattoos

Not Just Saturday Mornings

☆ What do the Flintstones, the Jetsons, Looney Tunes, Tiny Toons, Chester Cheetah, the Pink Panther, and Trolls have in common? They all have their own cartoon shows and movies and are all featured in their own **temporary tattoos**. Each package has at least two detailed tattoos in full color. The normal retail price is $3.99 per package, but this supplier wants you to have it at a 25% discount.

Send: $3.00 postage & handling

Ask For: Specify which cartoon character you want

Mail To: World of Tattoos
Box 304
Allenhurst, NJ 07711

☆ There's a new hobby out of Hawaii that's heading toward the mainland with the force of a tidal wave. Pog mania—the pastime of collecting and playing with milk-bottle caps—is a fad of huge proportions. **Pogs**, as they are called by Hawaiians, are flat cardboard or plastic discs with assorted design imprints. Send for this collector's set of sample pogs and instructions for a pog game.

Send: $1.00 postage & handling

Ask For: Sample pogs and game instructions

Mail To: Bittersweet
P.O. Box 10586
Honolulu, HI 96816

☆ Now you can take a stand with your favorite sport by displaying two different team players in a **two-card Top Load display stand**. This wooden base is created to fit two standard-size sportscards side by side in protective acrylic. With your stand you will also receive two protective cases and two complimentary sportscards with your choice of sport.

Send: $1.50 postage and handling

Ask For: Top Load wood and acrylic display with two free cards—specify baseball, basketball, football, or hockey

Mail To: The 10th Inning
P.O. Box 5902
Knoxville, TN 37928

Math Worksheet
It Adds Up

☆ Putt-Putt™ Golf wants to make sure your score adds up to an "A" with this five-page Buster Ball "Math for the Fun of It" **activity pack**. There are 18 word problems that are geared to elementary school-age youngsters and designed to emphasize critical thinking, reading, addition, and subtraction. Follow Buster Ball and everything adds up to fun.

Send: $2.00 postage & handling

Ask For: Math worksheets

Mail To: Putt-Putt Golf Freebies Offer
Box 35237
Fayetteville, NC 28303

CARTOON CONVENTION

☆ Batman, Rocky and Bullwinkle, the Marvel superheroes, Felix the Cat, Betty Boop, and Popeye can be seen on TV, in movies, and in the comics—and now they can be seen with you. You can boop, boop-a-doop with Betty, kapow! with Batman, and sail the seas with Popeye when you send for a set of **temporary tattoos** that are non-toxic, easy to apply, and easy to remove. Each package has at least two safe and colorful tattoos. You can save 25% off the normal retail price of $3.99 when you order from this special offer.

Send: $3.00 postage & handling
Ask For: Specify which character you want
Mail To: World of Tattoos
Box 304
Allenhurst, NJ 07711

☆ Trolls are the hottest things around. They even have their own cartoon show. Now you can get your own trio of **troll key chains**. Standing about 1-1/2" tall, these characters can also be used as pencil toppers by simply detaching the chain. Each has long hair that sticks up in one of six bright colors.

Send: $2.00 postage & handling for three
Ask For: Troll trio
Mail To: E Street Gifts
716 N. Ventura Rd., Suite 308
Oxnard, CA 93030

Troll Dolls

Trolling Along

Several pro teams expressed particular interest in keeping *Freebies* readers informed about their teams and have prepared special fan packages.

☆ If you're a hockey fanatic who loves to cheer the Chicago Blackhawks, you can "puck" up some insight into the Blackhawk hockey season by sending for a free **Blackhawk fan package**. You'll score lots of information when you receive a palm-size game schedule, three postcard-size pictures of individual team players, and a decal.

Hockey Fan Package

The Right Puck

Send: A long SASE

Ask For: Chicago Blackhawk fan package

Mail To: Chicago Blackhawks
Fan Package
1800 W. Madison St.
Chicago, IL 60612

Seventh-Inning Stretch

☆ For a detailed update on baseball's most famous franchise, catch a **sample copy of** *Yankees Magazine*. This official publication, focusing on the New York Yankees, is 86 pages packed full of color action photos and feature stories. You will save $1.00 off the normal retail price of $3.00. Plus, *Yankees Magazine* is sure to give you scores of informative and entertaining insight into this celebrated baseball team.

Send: $2.00 postage & handling

Ask For: *Yankees Magazine*

Mail To: Yankees Magazine
Yankee Stadium
Freebies Dept.
Bronx, NY 10451

☆ What a capital idea for hockey fans all over the United States: a free **Washington Capitals fan package** that includes all kinds of information about the hockey team headquartered at the nation's capital. The free packet contains a team history, statistics, a brochure of souvenirs, a pocket schedule, and a 3-3/4" x 7-1/2" bumper sticker.

Team Fan Package
A Capital Idea

Send: A long SASE

Ask For: Washington Capitals fan package

Mail To: Washington Capitals
U.S. Air Arena
Landover, MD 20785
Attn: Fan Package

☆ Slam dunk your way through history with this informative **booklet about the history of basketball.** Learn exciting facts and trivia about the game that began with a peach basket for a hoop in this booklet titled *Basketball Was Born Here.* You'll also get a color brochure about the Basketball Hall of Fame located in Springfield, Massachusetts, the home of basketball.

BASKETBALL JONES WAS HERE

Send: $1.00 postage & handling, plus a long SASE

Ask For: Basketball Was Born Here booklet

Mail To: Basketball Hall of Fame
1150 West Columbus Ave.
Springfield, MA 01101

Bumper Sticker

Year- **Round Hoops**

☆ Did you know the United States Basketball League (USBL) season starts around Memorial Day and runs until school starts in the fall? Considering the USBL has been operating successfully since its inception in 1985, there seems to be quite a few basketball fans who no longer have the summertime blues. Show your support for the USBL by ordering its red, white, and blue **bumper sticker.**

Send: 50¢ postage & handling

Ask For: United States Basketball League bumper sticker

Mail To: United States Basketball League
P.O. Box 211
Milford, CT 06460

Cotton Bowl Sticker

Gridiron Greats

☆ If you are a fan of the Cotton Bowl, then you need your own free 3-7/8" x 2-7/8" Mobil **Cotton Bowl sticker** emblazoned with the bowl game's official logo. The annual event pits the Southwestern Conference champs against a highly ranked team. Recent Cotton Bowls have featured the Texas Longhorns, the Texas A&M Aggies, the Miami Hurricanes, and the Florida State Seminoles.

Send: A long SASE

Ask For: Mobil Cotton Bowl Classic sticker

Mail To: Mobil Cotton Bowl Classic
P.O. Box 569420
Dallas, TX 75356-9420

☆ Pro football fans know that the Hall of Fame is located in Canton, Ohio. But why? It's because the first professional team was the Canton Bulldogs, formed in 1920. This and other football information is contained in the Pro Football Hall of Fame Enshrinees **roster and fact sheet**. The roster tells you when each player or coach was enshrined, lists their many accomplishments, and provides appropriate statistical information.

Roster and Fact Sheet

On Any Sunday

Send: A long SASE

Ask For: Roster of Enshrinees and Fact Sheet

Mail To: Pro Football Hall of Fame
2121 George Halas Dr., NW
Canton, OH 44708

☆ College football began in 1869 when Rutgers University beat Princeton, 6-4. Certainly the game has changed since then. The College Football Hall of Fame has documented all such changes plus commemorated all the top players, famous coaches, and historic moments. You can celebrate the sport by ordering a **College Football Hall of Fame magnet** for your bulletin board or refrigerator door.

Magnet
The College Game

Send: 75¢ postage & handling

Ask For: College Football Hall of Fame Magnet

Mail To: College Football Hall of Fame
Kings Island, OH 45034

...ns and then there are fanatics. If you love football, most likely ...to the second category. No matter how many magazines or ...rs you read, there's never enough information on your favorite ...his is especially true if you support a team located in any city other ...ur hometown. Keep up on your favorite NFL team with the club's ...al newspaper. It will provide in-depth information on your favorite ...ers and coaches, along with predictions, statistics, and schedules. If ...u're lucky, maybe your favorite team is included in the following list.

Chicago Bears

Once the famed Monsters of the Midway, the Bears are rebuilding under the watchful eye of new coach Dave Wannstedt. Despite the record, there's no one more devoted than a fan of Da' Bears.

Send: $1.25 postage & handling

Ask For: *Bear Report* sample issue

Mail To: Circulation Dept.
The Royle Group
112 Market St.
Sun Prairie, WI 53590

Green Bay Packers

The Pack is definitely back. With Sterling Sharpe setting pass receiving records and big Reggie White anchoring the Packers defense, Green Bay coach Mike Holmgren has put together a formidable NFC Central Division team.

Send: $1.25 postage & handling

Ask For: *Packer Report* sample copy

Mail To: Circulation Dept.
The Royle Group
112 Market St.
Sun Prairie, WI 53590

Dallas Cowboys

The Cowboys were once known as America's team. After Jimmy Johnson coached them to the 1993 Super Bowl Championship, the Cowboys once again have a national following. It sure doesn't hurt to have players like Troy Aikman, Michael Irvin, and Emmitt Smith.

Send: $2.25 postage & handling

Ask For: *Dallas Cowboys Official Weekly* sample issue

Mail To: Dallas Cowboys Weekly
Cowboys Center
One Cowboys Parkway
Irving, TX 75063-4727

Pittsburgh Steelers

One of the most successful tea[...] Super Bowl history, Pittsburg[...] longer has the Steel Curtain, b[...] does have Rod Woodson [...] defense. The Steelers also hav[...] fine coach in Bill Cowher.

Send: $1.00 postage & handling

Ask For: *Steelers Digest* sample copy

Mail To: Curtis Publishing Company
P.O. Box 526600
Miami, FL 33152

Miami Dolphins

What do the Dolphins have besides a record as the last team to finish an NFL season undefeated? They have one of the most successful coaches in the history of pro football—Don Shula. They also have a young defense and an awesome passing game.

Send: $1.00 postage & handling

Ask For: *Dolphin Digest* sample copy

Mail To: Curtis Publishing Company
P.O. Box 526600
Miami, FL 33152

Eagles

...y have left, but the ... flying high under ...otite. Despite recent ...ges, Philadelphia is a ...contended with in the ...n NFC East division.

$1.00 postage & handling

or: *Eagles Digest* sample copy

To: Curtis Publishing Company
P.O. Box 526600
Miami, FL 33152

New Orleans Saints

Mardi Gras isn't just once a year. It comes to the Superdome any time the Saints take the field. With fan support like that, it's no wonder Jim Mora has been so successful during his eight seasons with New Orleans.

Send: $1.00 postage & handling

Ask For: *Saints Digest* sample copy

Mail To: Curtis Publishing Company
P.O. Box 526600
Miami, FL 33152

New York Giants

Some people suggested the only reason Dan Reeves won in Denver was because of John Elway. He's proved the skeptics wrong since taking over the Giants.

Send: $3.50 postage & handling

Ask For: *The Giants Newsweekly* sample issue

Mail To: Pro Publishing, Inc.
P.O. Box 816
Red Bank, NJ 07701

☆ Most professional sports franchises have free materials, such as season schedules and ticket information, that they give away to enthusiastic fans. Some teams even give away neat packages that may contain stickers, photos, fan club info, catalogs, and more.

To get these great gifts, all you need to do is write the name of your favorite team on your request card and ask for a fan package. We've compiled the addresses of all the professional baseball, basketball, football, and hockey teams. Although not all teams require it, we recommend you send a long, self-addressed, stamped envelope (SASE) to help speed your request.

Here's another tip: If you want to contact a specific player on your favorite team, address the envelope to his attention. Keep in mind that because of the high volume of fan mail each team receives, it may take eight weeks or more to get a response. So be a good sport!

AMERICAN LEAGUE BASEBALL TEAMS

Baltimore Orioles
Memorial Stadium
Baltimore, MD 21218

Boston Red Sox
4 Yawkey Way
Boston, MA 02115

California Angels
P.O. Box 2000
Anaheim, CA 92803

Chicago White Sox
333 W. 35th St.
Chicago, IL 60616

Cleveland Indians
Cleveland Stadium
Cleveland, OH 44114

Detroit Tigers
Public Relations
2121 Trumbull Ave.
Detroit, MI 48216

Kansas City Royals
P.O. Box 419969
Kansas City, MO 64141

Milwaukee Brewers
201 S. 46th St.
Milwaukee, WI 53214

Minnesota Twins
501 Chicago Ave. South
Minneapolis, MN 55415

New York Yankees
Yankee Stadium
Bronx, NY 10451

Oakland Athletics
Oakland Coliseum
Oakland, CA 94621

Seattle Mariners
P.O. Box 4100
Seattle, WA 98104

Texas Rangers
P.O. Box 90111
Arlington, TX 76010

Toronto Blue Jays
Sky Dome
300 Bremmer Blvd., Suite 3200
Toronto, Ontario, Canada
MSV 3B3
(Postage to Canada is 40¢)

NATIONAL LEAGUE BASEBALL TEAMS

Atlanta Braves
P.O. Box 4064
Atlanta, GA 30302

Chicago Cubs
Wrigley Field
1060 W. Addison St.
Chicago, IL 60613

Cincinnati Reds
100 Riverfront Stadium
Cincinnati, OH 45202

Colorado Rockies
1700 Broadway, Suite 2100
Denver, CO 80290

Florida Marlins
100 NE 3rd Ave.
Ft. Lauderdale, FL 33301

Houston Astros
P.O. Box 288
Houston, TX 77001-0288

Los Angeles Dodgers
1000 Elysian Park Ave.
Los Angeles, CA 90012

Montreal Expos
P.O. Box 500, Station M
Montreal, Quebec, Canada
HIV 3P2
(Postage to Canada is 40¢)

New York Mets
Shea Stadium
Flushing, NY 11368

Philadelphia Phillies
Veteran Stadium
P.O. Box 7575
Philadelphia, PA 19101

Pittsburgh Pirates
Public Relations
P.O. Box 7000
Pittsburgh, PA 15212

St. Louis Cardinals
250 Stadium Plaza
St. Louis, MO 63102

San Diego Padres
P.O. Box 2000
San Diego, CA 92102

San Francisco Giants
Candlestick Park
San Francisco, CA 94124

Atlanta Hawks
1 CNN Center
South Tower, Suite 405
Atlanta, GA 30303

Boston Celtics
151 Merrimac St., 5th Fl.
Boston, MA 02114

Charlotte Hornets
Fan Mail
Hive Dr.
Charlotte, NC 28217

Chicago Bulls
980 N. Michigan Ave., Suite 1600
Chicago, IL 60611-4501

Cleveland Cavaliers
Community Relations
2923 Streetsboro Rd.
Richfield, OH 44286

Dallas Mavericks
Reunion Arena
777 Sports St.
Dallas, TX 75207

Denver Nuggets
1635 Clay St.
Denver, CO 80204

Detroit Pistons
2 Championship Dr.
Auburn Hills, MI 48326

Golden State Warriors
Oakland Coliseum Arena
Oakland, CA 94621-1995

Houston Rockets
P.O. Box 272349
Houston, TX 77277

Indiana Pacers
300 E. Market St.
Indianapolis, IN 46204

Los Angeles Clippers
L.A. Memorial Sports Arena
3939 S. Figueroa
Los Angeles, CA 90037

Los Angeles Lakers
Great Western Forum
P.O. Box 10
Inglewood, CA 90306

Miami Heat
Miami Arena
Miami, FL 33136-4102

Milwaukee Bucks
1001 N. 4th St.
Milwaukee, WI 53203

Minnesota Timberwolves
600 1st Ave. North
Minneapolis, MN 55403

New Jersey Nets
Brendan Byrne Arena
East Rutherford, NJ 07073

New York Knicks
Madison Square Garden
4 Penn Plaza
New York, NY 10001

Orlando Magic
1 Magic Pl.
Orlando Arena
Orlando, FL 32801

Philadelphia 76ers
Veteran Stadium
P.O. Box 25040
Philadelphia, PA 19147

Phoenix Suns
P.O. Box 1369
Phoenix, AZ 85001

Portland Trail Blazers
Lloyd Bldg., Suite 950
700 NE Multnomah St.
Portland, OR 97232

Sacramento Kings
1 Sports Pkwy.
Sacramento, CA 95834

Seattle Supersonics
C-Box 900911
Seattle, WA 98109

Washington Bullets
Capital Centre
Landover, MD 20785

San Antonio Spurs
600 E. Market St., Suite 102
San Antonio, TX 78205

Utah Jazz
301 W. South Temple
Salt Lake City, UT 84101

AMERICAN CONFERENCE FOOTBALL TEAMS

Buffalo Bills
1 Bills Dr.
Orchard Park, NY 14127

Indianapolis Colts
7001 W. 56th St.
Indianapolis, IN 46224-0100

New York Jets
100 Fulton Ave.
Hempstead, NY 11550

Cincinnati Bengals
200 Riverfront Stadium
Cincinnati, OH 45202

Kansas City Chiefs
1 Arrowhead Dr.
Kansas City, MO 64129

Pittsburgh Steelers
Three Rivers Stadium
300 Stadium Circle
Pittsburgh, PA 15212

Cleveland Browns
Cleveland Stadium
Cleveland, OH 44114

Los Angeles Raiders
332 Center St.
El Segundo, CA 90245

San Diego Chargers
Jack Murphy Stadium
9449 Friars Rd.
San Diego, CA 92108

Denver Broncos
13655 E. Dove Valley Pkwy.
Englewood, CO 80112

Miami Dolphins
Joe Robbie Stadium
2269 NW 199th St.
Miami, FL 33056

Seattle Seahawks
11220 NE 53rd St.
Kirkland, WA 98033

Houston Oilers
6910 Fannin St.
Houston, TX 77030

New England Patriots
Foxboro Stadium—Rte. 1
Foxboro, MA 02035

NATIONAL CONFERENCE FOOTBALL TEAMS

Atlanta Falcons
Suwanee Rd. at I-85
Suwanee, GA 30174

Chicago Bears
Halas Hall
250 N. Washington Rd.
Lake Forest, IL 60045

Dallas Cowboys
Cowboys Center
1 Cowboys Pkwy.
Irving, TX 75063-4727

Detroit Lions
1200 Featherstone Rd.
Pontiac, MI 48057

Green Bay Packers
1265 Lombardi Ave.
Green Bay, WI 54304

Los Angeles Rams
2327 W. Lincoln Ave.
Anaheim, CA 92801

Minnesota Vikings
9520 Viking Dr.
Eden Prairie, MN 55344

New Orleans Saints
1500 Poydras St.
New Orleans, LA 70003

New York Giants
Giants Stadium
East Rutherford, NJ 07073

Philadelphia Eagles
Broad St. & Pattison Ave.
Philadelphia, PA 19148

Phoenix Cardinals
P.O. Box 888
Phoenix, AZ 85001-0888

San Francisco 49ers
4949 Centennial Blvd.
Santa Clara, CA 95054-1229

Tampa Bay Buccaneers
1 Buccaneer Pl.
Tampa, FL 33607

Washington Redskins
P.O. Box 17247
Dulles International Airport
Washington, DC 20041

NATIONAL HOCKEY LEAGUE

The Mighty Ducks/Disney
Sports Enterprises
P.O. Box 61077
Anaheim, CA 92803-6177

Boston Bruins
Boston Garden
150 Causeway St.
Boston, MA 02114

Buffalo Sabres
Memorial Auditorium
140 Main St.
Buffalo, NY 14202

Calgary Flames
P.O. Box 1540
Station M
Calgary, Alberta, Canada
T2P 3B9
(Postage to Canada is 40¢)

Chicago Black Hawks
Chicago Stadium
1800 W. Madison
Chicago, IL 60612

Detroit Red Wings
600 Civic Center Dr.
Detroit, MI 48226

Edmonton Oilers
Northlands Coliseum
7424-118 Ave.
Edmonton, Alberta,
Canada T5B 4M9
(Postage to Canada is 40¢)

Hartford Whalers
242 Trumbull St.
Hartford, CT 06103

Los Angeles Kings
c/o Individual Player
P.O. Box 17013
Inglewood, CA 90308

Minnesota North Stars
Met Center
7901 Cedar Ave. South
Bloomington, MN 55425

Montreal Canadiens
2313 St. Katherine West
Montreal, Quebec, Canada
413H IN2
(Postage to Canada is 40¢)

New Jersey Devils
Fan Pack
P.O. Box 504
East Rutherford, NJ 07073

New York Islanders
Nassau Coliseum
Uniondale, NY 11553

New York Rangers
Public Relations
Madison Square Garden
4 Penn Plaza
New York, NY 10001

Philadelphia Flyers
The Spectrum-Pattison Pl.
Philadelphia, PA 15219

Pittsburgh Penguins
Civic Arena, Gate #7
Pittsburgh, PA 15219

Quebec Nordiques
Colisee de Quebec
2205 Avenue de Colisee
Quebec, Quebec, Canada
GIL 4W7
(Postage to Canada is 40¢)

San Jose Sharks
10 Almeden Blvd.
San Jose, CA 95113

St. Louis Blues
The Arena
5700 Oakland Ave.
St. Louis, MO 63110

Toronto Maple Leafs
Maple Leaf Gardens
60 Carlton St.
Toronto, Ontario, Canada
M5B ILI
(Postage to Canada is 40¢)

Vancouver Canucks
Pacific Coliseum
100 N. Renfrew St.
Vancouver, B.C., Canada
V5K 3N7
(Postage to Canada is 40¢)

Washington Capitals
Capital Centre
Landover, MD 20786

Winnipeg Jets
Winnipeg Arena
15-1430 Maroons Rd.
Winnipeg, Manitoba,
Canada R3G OL5
(Postage to Canada is 40¢)

PLACES TO GO!

Stars and fans are everywhere. You only need to know where to look. The *Freebies* staff has compiled a listing of some famous and not-so-famous places to visit across the country. Be sure to call ahead of time for hours and any admission costs.

Arizona

☆ **Flintstones' Bedrock City** is a theme park and RV campground featuring life-size Flintstone houses and your favorite characters from the prehistoric TV cartoon. Near the Grand Canyon on Grand Canyon Highway (Highway 64 and 180), Williams, AZ 86046. (602) 635-2600.

California

☆ The **Academy of Television Arts and Sciences Library** contains files, books, and archive materials from the entertainment industry. 5200 Lankershim Blvd., Suite 340, North Hollywood, CA 91601. (818) 752-1870.

☆ The **Margaret Herrick Library** and the **Academy Film Archive** are located at the Academy of Motion Picture Arts and Sciences Center for Motion Picture Study. Here you can find clipping files on over 60,000 films and over 50,000 people involved in the industry; 18,000 books, pamphlets, and periodicals; 5,000 scripts; 5 million still photographs; and over 12,000 films. 333 S. La Cienega Blvd., Beverly Hills, CA 90211. (310) 247-3000.

☆ The **University of California, Los Angeles, Theater Arts Library** is located at the UCLA campus in Westwood at 405 Hilgard Ave., Los Angeles, CA 90024. (310) 825-4880.

☆ The **University of Southern California's Cinema-TV Library** contains 60,000 clipping files on personalities, film, and TV, 10,000 scripts, a press book collection and audio- and videotapes. The library is located at USC's downtown campus; call (213) 740-8906.

☆ **The Lucy Museum** is a heart-shaped building at Universal Studios in Universal City that holds a collection of memorabilia for Lucille Ball fans, including Emmys, scripts, and costumes. 100 Universal City Plaza, Universal City, CA 91608. (818) 508-9600.

☆ **The Unknown Museum** in northern California has over 200 Mr. Potato Heads on display, including the history and evolution of the famous spud. The museum is open by appointment only. Write to The Unknown Museum, P.O. Box 1551, Mill Valley, CA 94942. (415) 383-2726.

☆ A museum designed to convey the spirit of the West, the **Gene Autry Western Heritage Museum** features displays like Buffalo Bill's firearms, costumes, and saddle and Annie Oakley's rifle and hat. Films and special effects add to the feeling of the Old West. 4700 Western Heritage Way, Griffith Park, Los Angeles, CA 90027. (213) 667-2000.

☆ The **Max Factor Museum of Beauty** showcases the use of makeup throughout Hollywood film history and features such interesting exhibits as the Kissing Machine, two sets of rubber lips that press together for the purpose of testing lipstick's staying power. 1666 N. Highland Ave., Hollywood, CA.

☆ Recent exhibits of original comic art can be found at the **Cartoon Art Museum**. Original art and autographed books are sold in the gift shop. 665 Third St., San Francisco, CA 94107.

☆ See the sets of some of your favorite movies at **Universal Studios**. The tour provides information on film history and the basics of movie making and special effects, and shows you the house from *Psycho* and sets from other movies. 100 Universal City Plaza, Universal City, CA 91608. (818) 508-9600.

☆ At the **Roy Rogers–Dale Evans Museum** you will find a 30,000-square-foot replica of a frontier fort and souvenirs of Roy Rogers's and Dale Evans's personal and professional lives. 15650 Seneca Rd., Victorville, CA 92392. (619) 243-4547.

☆ Visit L.A.'s only **Museum of Animation**. 8483 Melrose Ave., West Hollywood, CA 90069. Open Tuesday through Saturday, 12–7:30 P.M. and Sunday, 12–5 P.M.

Connecticut

☆ Fans of the circus and P. T. Barnum can learn circus history and view artifacts that cannot be seen anywhere else at **The Barnum Museum.** 820 Main St., Bridgeport, CT 06604.

District of Columbia

☆ The **Smithsonian Oz Exhibit** features a pair of ruby slippers, the Scarecrow costume, and an early draft of the *Wizard of Oz* script. Smithsonian Museum, Washington, DC.

Florida

☆ Take a tour to **The Beatles Room** in Miami where John Lennon slept during a 1964 concert tour. Highlights include Beatle portraits, wallpaper, and the actual toilet they used. Guests leave with complimentary souvenirs including John Lennon pillowcases and a keychain.

☆ See the handmade 1907 Model T prototype that Henry Ford gave to his friend Thomas Edison. The car is one of only three or four of its kind. **Edison's home** is open daily for guided tours. 2350 McGregor Blvd., Fort Myers, FL 33901.

☆ Take the **Disney-MGM Studios Theme Park Animation Tour**, where, from a glass-walled walkway, you can glimpse new animated films in the making. P.O. Box 10,000, Lake Buena,Vista, FL 32830-1000. (407) 824-4531.

Georgia

☆ In Atlanta, the birthplace of Coca-Cola, you can visit **The World of Coca-Cola,** which contains the drink's history and hundreds of advertising displays. Admission to the museum is $2.50 and includes all the Coke you can drink plus samples of 18 Coke flavors not available in North America. 55 Martin Luther King Dr., Atlanta, GA 30303-3505. (404) 676-5151.

Indiana

☆ **The Yellow Brick Road Gift Shop** features such *Wizard of Oz* memorabilia as a replica of the witch's castle on the mountain and autographed photos of the cast. Chesterson, IN. (219) 926-7048.

☆ Fairmount, Indiana, is where James Dean grew up and is buried. **Museum Days** is held on the weekend nearest the anniversary of Dean's death. Most of the events take place at Fairmount Museum on Washington Street. Dean's grave is at **Park Cemetery**.

Kansas

☆ Visit **Dorothy's House**, a replica of the farm in *The Wizard of Oz*. The house has a museum with the original miniature house used in the movie for the twister scene. The movie is shown daily. Liberal, KS. (316) 624-7624.

Kentucky

☆ **Kentucky Fried Chicken International Headquarters** is a small museum featuring plaques and honorary titles given to Colonel Sanders, as well as a wire sculpture of a hen laying a golden egg. Press a button and the hen turns and flaps her wings. 1441 Gardiner Lane, Louisville, KY 40232-2070. (502) 456-8300.

New York

☆ The **Lincoln Center Performing Arts Library** contains extensive information about performing arts and includes an archive. 111 Amsterdam Ave., New York, NY 10019. (212) 870-1630.

☆ The **Museum of Cartoon Art** holds a collection of over 60,000 original works and regularly features appearances by top cartoonists. Comly Ave, Rye Brook, NY 10573.

Ohio

☆ **The Center of Science and Industry** contains over 10,000 pieces of Cracker Jack memorabilia, including advertising, prizes, and premiums. 280 E. Broad St., Columbus, OH 43215. (614) 228-2674.

Pennsylvania

☆ Visit a replica of the Hershey factory at **Hershey Park and Botanical Gardens**. The park features rides and a trolley tour. 300 Park Blvd., Hershey, PA 17033. (800) 437-7439.

☆ Visit one of the factories that make Crayola crayons. During the one-hour **Crayola Product Tour** you will see the mixing, molding, labeling, and boxing process in action. Reservations are necessary and should be made months in advance. 1100 Church Lane, P.O. Box 431, Easton, PA 18044-0431. (A Crayola factory is also located in Winfield, Kansas.)

South Dakota

☆ See six acres of furnished life-size Flintstone houses, a dinosaur slide, a prehistoric train, and Mt. Rockmore at **Flintstones' Bedrock City**. Bring your camera and take pictures of Dino, Fred, Barney, Wilma, and Betty. Highway 16, P.O. Box 649, Custer, SD 57730. (605) 673-4079.

Tennessee

☆ Antique pistols, Remington bronzes, and more Johnny Cash memorabilia are on display at the **House of Cash**. Nashville, TN. (615) 824-5110.

☆ Visit a replica of Barbara Mandrell's bedroom at **Barbara Mandrell Country**. Nashville, TN. (615) 242-7800.

☆ **Opryland** offers a tour of the Grand Ole Opry as well as some wild rides. Nashville, TN. (615) 889-6700.

☆ **Minnie Pearl's Museum**. Nashville, TN. (615) 889-6700.

☆ View mementos owned by the late Conway Twitty at **Twitty City**. Nashville, TN. (615) 822-6650.

☆ **Country Music Hall of Fame**. Nashville, TN. (615) 255-5333.

☆ **Museum of Beverage Containers and Advertising**. Nashville, TN. (615) 859-5236.

Wisconsin

☆ Visit the **Houdini Historical Center** in the magician's hometown of Appleton, Wisconsin. The center contains the world's largest collection of Houdini memorabilia, including the oversized milk can used in one of his famous escapes. Outagamie Museum, 330 E. College Ave., Appleton, WI 54911. (414) 733-8445.

FREE TICKETS TO TV SHOWS AND NETWORK ADDRESSES

Many television shows have live studio audiences, and tickets are free for the asking. But a lot of shows are in high demand and may be crowded. For tickets and information, contact the organizations below. Be sure to ask if there are any age restrictions, as some shows do not admit youngsters under 16.

☆ **Audiences Unlimited**
(independent and studio shows)
100 Universal City Plaza, Building 153
Universal City, CA 91608
818/506-0067

•Call and they can tell you what's filming in the next two weeks;

•or send a SASE and request a calendar of shows at least a month in advance for the month you'll be in town;

•or send a SASE with the date and number of tickets you want, and they'll send you what's available;

•or send a SASE with the exact show, date, and number of tickets you want, and they'll send them as long as they're available,

☆ For free tickets to shows on ABC, CBS, and NBC, call or write ahead of time for information on what shows will be taped while you are visiting New York or Los Angeles. When you call or write ask for "Guest Tickets."

ABC
4151 Prospect Ave.
Los Angeles, CA 90027
310/557-7777
or
77 W. 66th St.
New York, NY 10023

CBS
7800 Beverly Blvd.
Los Angeles, CA 90036
213/852-2624
or
51 W. 52nd St.
New York, NY 10019

NBC
3000 W. Alameda Ave.
Burbank, CA 91523
818/840-4444
or
30 Rockefeller Plaza
New York, NY 10112

Fox Broadcasting Co.
10201 W. Pico Blvd.
Los Angeles, CA 90035

Movie Studios

Columbia Pictures (Sony
Pictures Entertainment, Inc.)
10202 W. Washington Blvd.
Culver City, CA 90232

Fox, Inc.
10201 W. Pico Blvd.
Los Angeles, CA 90035

MGM-Pathé
Communications Co.
10000 W. Washington Blvd.
Culver City, CA 90232

Orion Pictures Corp.
1888 Century Park East
Los Angeles, CA 90067

Paramount
Communications, Inc.
5555 Melrose Ave.
Los Angeles, CA 90038

Touchstone Pictures
500 S. Buena Vista St.
Burbank, CA 91521

Twentieth Century-Fox
P.O. Box 900
Beverly Hills, CA 90213

Universal Pictures
100 Universal City Plaza
Universal City, CA 91608

Warner Brothers, Inc.
400 Warner Blvd.
Burbank, CA 91522

Record Companies

CBS Records, Inc.
51 W. 52nd St.
New York, NY 10019

Capitol-EMI Music, Inc.
1750 N. Vine St.
Hollywood, CA 90028

EMI
810 Seventh Ave., 8th Floor
New York, NY 10019

Elektra Entertainment
(and Warner Music
International)
75 Rockefeller Plaza
New York, NY 10019

MCA Records
70 Universal City Plaza
Universal City, CA 91608

Motown Record Co.
6255 Sunset Blvd.
17th Floor
Los Angeles, CA 90028

RCA Records, Inc.
P.O. Box 126
405 Tarrytown Rd.
Suite 335
Elmsford, NY 10523

SBK Records
1290 Avenue of the
Americas
New York, NY 10104

The Soaps

All My Children
ABC-TV
77 W. 66th St.
New York, NY 10023

Days of Our Lives
NBC-TV
3000 W. Alameda Ave.
Burbank, CA 91523

One Life to Live
ABC-TV
77 W. 66th St.
New York, NY 10023

Another World
NBC-TV
30 Rockefeller Plaza
New York, NY 10112

General Hospital
ABC-TV
4151 Prospect Ave.
Hollywood, CA 90027

The Young & the Restless
CBS-TV
7800 Beverly Blvd.
Los Angeles, CA 90036

As the World Turns
CBS-TV
51 W. 52nd St.
New York, NY 10019

Guiding Light
CBS-TV
222 E. 44th St.
New York, NY 10017

The Bold & the Beautiful
CBS-TV
7800 Beverly Blvd.
Los Angeles, CA 90036

Loving
ABC-TV
77 W. 66th St.
New York, NY 10023

CLOSING CREDITS!

Who could resist being starstruck by the very idea of television and movie making in Hollywood and all the glamour surrounding it? If you are drawn to the screen or stage but are just a bit too shy in front of the camera, a job behind the scenes may be for you. Or, if you are just curious about what some of the words mean in the closing credits, read on. The following is a list of selected entertainment industry jobs that may not be familiar to you.

Gaffer The chief electrician, supervises all lighting and staff.

Best Boy Second electrician, responsible for ordering and maintaining electrical equipment.

Key Grip Foreperson of the grip team, moves equipment to and from sets and locations and makes repairs as needed.

Dolly Grip Pushes the camera dollies during shots.

Focus Puller Assistant cameraperson, manipulates the camera during shooting by adjusting focus.

Boom Operator Member of the production sound team, maneuvers the long "fishpole" mike, keeping it in the range of the actors but out of sight of the camera.

Foley Artist Re-creates sounds (e.g., rain, footsteps, wind) in a foley sound studio.

Negative Cutter Matches the editor's final cut with an untouched original and carefully edits it to fit, creating a master negative.

Go-fer Can work in any of the behind-the-scenes departments, running errands and tying up loose ends.

FREE   FREE   FREE

Something for nothing!! Hundreds of dollars worth of items in each issue of **FREEBIES Magazine.** Five times a year, for over 14 years, each issue features at least 100 FREE and low-postage-&-handling-only offers. Useful, informative and fun items. Household information, catalogs, recipes, health/medical information, toys for the kids, samples of everything from tea bags to jewelry—every offer of every issue is yours for FREE, or for a small postage and handling charge (never more than $2.00)!

Have you purchased a "Free Things" book before—only to find that the items were unavailable? That won't happen with FREEBIES—all of our offers are authenticated (and verified for accuracy) with the suppliers!

- -

☑ **YES - Send me 5 issues for only $4.95**
(save $4.00 off the regular subscription rate!)

☐ Payment Enclosed, or Charge my   ☐ VISA   ☐ MasterCard

Card Number _ _ _ _ _ _ _ _ _ _ _ _ _ _ _ _   Exp. Date _ _ _ _

Name_____

Address_____

City_____ State _____ Zip_____

Daytime Phone #

( )_____

(in case we have a question about your subscription)

Send to: FREEBIES MAGAZINE/FANS Offer
1135 Eugenia Place, P.O. Box 5025, Carpinteria, CA 93014